★ IT'S MY STATE! ★

PENNSYLVANIA

Joyce Hart

Richard Hantula

mc Marshall Cavendish
Benchmark

New York

Other Marshall Cavendish Offices:
Marshall Cavendish International (Asia) Private Limited, 1 New Industrial Road, Singapore 536196 •
Marshall Cavendish International (Thailand) Co Ltd. 253 Asoke, 12th Flr, Sukhumvit 21 Road, Klongtoey Nua, Wattana, Bangkok 10110, Thailand • Marshall Cavendish (Malaysia) Sdn Bhd, Times Subang, Lot 46, Subang Hi-Tech Industrial Park, Batu Tiga, 40000 Shah Alam, Selangor Darul Ehsan, Malaysia

Marshall Cavendish is a trademark of Times Publishing Limited

All websites were available and accurate when this book was sent to press.

Library of Congress Cataloging-in-Publication Data
Hart, Joyce, 1954-
      Pennsylvania / Joyce Hart and Richard Hantula. — 2nd ed.
         p. cm. — (It's my state!)
      Includes index.
      ISBN 978-1-60870-058-5
      1. Pennsylvania—Juvenile literature. I. Hantula, Richard. II. Title.
   F149.3.H37 2011
   974.8—dc22   2010003931

Second Edition developed for Marshall Cavendish Benchmark by RJF Publishing LLC (www.RJFpublishing.com)
Series Designer, Second Edition: Tammy West/Westgraphix LLC

All maps, illustrations, and graphics © Marshall Cavendish Corporation. Maps and artwork on pages 6, 42, 43, 75, 76, and back cover by Christopher Santoro. Map and graphics on pages 8 and 39 by Westgraphix LLC.

The photographs in this book are used by permission and through the courtesy of:
Front cover: Rena Schild and Sonya Etchison (inset)/Shutterstock.
Alamy: Daniel Dempster Photography, 9; Images-USA, 11, 56; Peter Steiner, 15; North Wind Picture Archives, 22, 28; H. Mark Weidman Photography, 36, 45, 66; Philip Scalia, 47; Frank Tozier, 57; Frank Paul, 65; Michael Ventura, 71 (inset), 72. **Getty Images:** Art Wolfe, 4; Dave King, 5 (top); © Matt Kazmierski, 10; Chuck Pefley, 12; Raymond Gehman/National Geographics, 13; H. Mark Weidman, 16 (top), 62, 74; Stephen J. Krasemann, 16 (bottom); Adam Jones, 18 (left); Taylor S. Kennedy/National Geographic, 18 (right); William Thomas Cain, 20, 40; Three Lions/Hulton Archive, 24; Kean Collection/Hulton Archive, 26; Stock Montage/Hulton Archive, 27; Buyenlarge/Hulton Archive, 30; Library of Congress/Hulton Archive, 32; New York Times Co./Hulton Archive, 33; Hulton Archive, 38; Superstock, 48; Harry How, 49 (top); Matthew Stockman, 49 (bottom); Jeff Swensen, 50; Rich Pilling/Major League Baseball, 51; Heather Weston, 63; Jeffrey Coolidge, 68 (top); Ken Lucas/Visuals Unlimited, 68 (bottom); Adam Crowley, 71 (Independence Hall); Mike Stahl, 73. **Shutterstock:** Caitlin Mirra, 5 (bottom); Delmas Lehman, 14; Geoffrey Kuchera, 19; Jerry Zitterman, 46; Dobresum, 52; BenC, 55; Elena Elisseeva, 60; Semen Lixodeev, 69. **U.S. Fish and Wildlife Service:** 17.

Printed in Malaysia (T).
135642

CONTENTS

State Tree: Eastern Hemlock

The eastern hemlock is an evergreen tree that can grow to be more than 100 feet (30 meters) tall. It thrives in almost every area of Pennsylvania. The early settlers used the wood to build their wagons, cabins, and furniture.

State Bird: Ruffed Grouse

The ruffed grouse is a plump, reddish brown bird. It can grow to be up to 19 inches (48 centimeters) long with a wingspan of up to 25 inches (64 cm). It spends a lot of time on the ground, making it easy for hunters to find. Many early inhabitants of Pennsylvania hunted the grouse for food.

State Flower: Mountain Laurel

The Pennsylvania legislature could not decide between the pink azalea and the mountain laurel as the state flower. In 1933, the choice was left to the wife of Governor Gifford Pinchot. She selected the mountain laurel, a woodland evergreen shrub with white and pink blossoms that grows in Pennsylvania forests.

State Dog: Great Dane

Great Danes are good hunting and guard dogs. Brought over from England, they were very popular with early settlers. In 1965, the state legislature honored the Great Dane's strength and loyalty by making it Pennsylvania's official dog. A portrait of William Penn (Pennsylvania's founder) together with his Great Dane hangs in the governor's reception room in the State Capitol.

State Fossil: *Phacops rana*

More than 300 million years ago, most of Pennsylvania was under water. As a result, many of the state's fossils are sea creatures, such as the *Phacops rana*. This creature was a kind of trilobite. Trilobites were relatives of horseshoe crabs, insects, and spiders and were among the first living things on earth known to have eyes. Trilobite fossils are often found in Pennsylvania.

State Flagship: U.S. Brig *Niagara*

This large warship took part in the Battle of Lake Erie, an 1813 fight between the United States and Great Britain during the War of 1812. The original U.S. Brig *Niagara* eventually sank, but it was raised and reconstructed in 1913. Later, a copy of the original ship was built. Today, it is a sailing school where students are the boat's crew on trips all over the Great Lakes.

5

PENNSYLVANIA

Lake Erie

Presque Isle

Erie

Allegheny River

St. Marys

Pittsburgh

Ohio River

Punxsutawney

Indiana

Allegheny Mountains

Altoona

Monongahela River

Fort Neccessity National Battlefield

Mount Davis

Tuscarora Mountains

Tuscarora River

Gettysburg National Military Park

Juniata River

Appalachian Mountains

Blue Mountains

Harrisburg

Susquehanna River

Scranton

Wilkes-Barre

Pocono Mountains

Delaware River

Blue Mountains

Allentown

Reading

Hershey

Lancaster

Valley Forge National Historical Park

Philadelphia

N

W   E

S

The Keystone State

Located in the eastern part of the United States, Pennsylvania is called the Keystone State. A keystone is a central stone in an arch. It holds the arch together. Pennsylvania got the name for two reasons. First, it was centrally located among the thirteen British colonies that combined to form the United States in the eighteenth century. Second, it played an important role in holding together the newly formed nation.

Today, Pennsylvania is a medium-size state in area. Its land area of 44,817 square miles (116,075 square kilometers) gives it a rank of thirty-second among the fifty U.S. states. But Pennsylvania ranks sixth among the states in population. The city of Philadelphia has more than 1.4 million people, making it the sixth-biggest city in the country. Pittsburgh, the state's second-largest city, has a population of about 300,000 people. The third-biggest city, with more than 100,000 people, is Allentown. Pennsylvania is divided into sixty-seven counties. Harrisburg, the state capital, is located in Dauphin County, in the east-central part of the state.

Quick Facts

PENNSYLVANIA BORDERS

North	New York
	Lake Erie
South	Delaware
	Maryland
	West Virginia
East	New York
	New Jersey
West	Ohio
	West Virginia

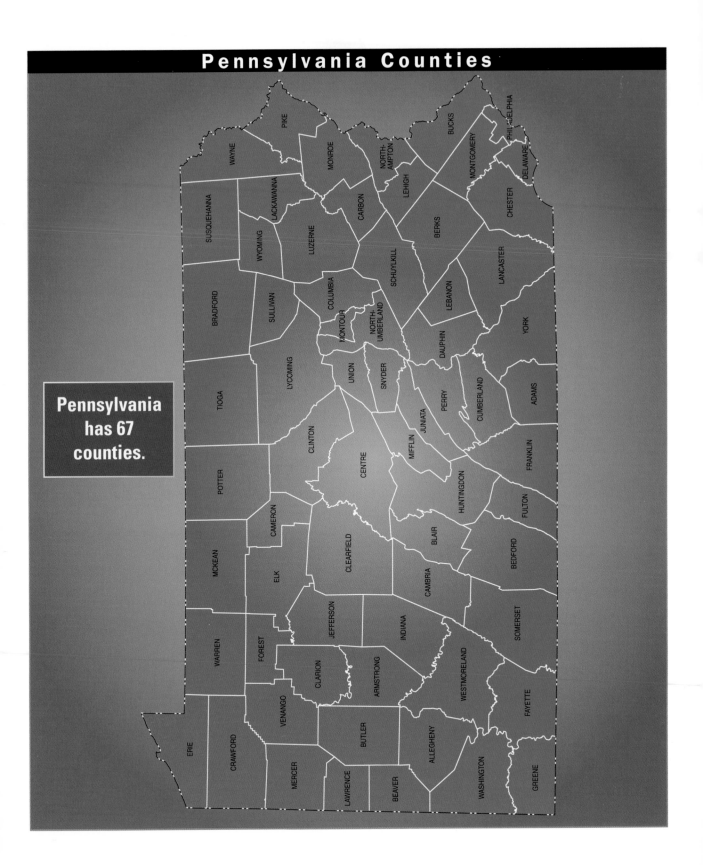

Pennsylvania has 67 counties.

The Landscape

Pennsylvania has a varied landscape, created by powerful geological forces. Tectonic plates, the huge floating layers of rock that make up the earth's surface, are continuously moving and crashing into each other. Millions of years ago, this activity formed mountain chains across parts of North America. Volcanoes and earthquakes further changed the landscape. Then, during the last Ice Age, a period that ended some ten thousand years ago, huge masses of moving ice, called glaciers, covered much of North America. This included the northern portion of present-day Pennsylvania. As the glaciers moved, rivers, valleys, and lakes were carved into the landscape. Through the years, wind, water, and other natural forces continued to shape the land. As a result, Pennsylvania's landscape today includes flat plains, gently rolling hills, valleys, and mountain chains.

The northwestern corner of the state is part of the Great Lakes Plain, which hugs the shores of Lake Erie. Lake Erie is one of the five Great Lakes and, in area, is the eleventh-largest lake in the world. The Great Lakes Plain is a relatively flat strip of land. The city of Erie is located here. With about 100,000 people, it is Pennsylvania's major port on the lake.

Presque Isle State Park includes a beautiful shoreline on Lake Erie.

CITY OF BRIDGES

Pittsburgh lies in the northern foothills of the Alleghenies, where the Monongahela and Allegheny rivers come together to form the Ohio River. According to a recent count, it has the most bridges of any city in the world.

The Fort Pitt Bridge across the Monongahela River is one of many bridges in Pittsburgh.

The edge of the plain gives way to the Appalachian Plateau, sometimes called the Allegheny Plateau in this region. A plateau is a mass of land that rises above the land surrounding it. Its sides often look like steep walls. Some plateaus are flat along the top, but the Appalachian Plateau has a rather rugged top. The Appalachian Plateau covers most of the western and northern portions of the state and is the location of many state parks and forests, as well as a national forest. Relatively few people live in this region, but the area is famous for its deposits of coal and oil.

The Appalachian Plateau gradually increases in height and becomes part of the Appalachian Mountains—a large chain of mountains that runs from southeastern Canada down to central Alabama. Many geologists believe this mountain range is one of the oldest in the world. More than 200 million years ago, the Appalachian Mountains were more than 15,000 feet (4,500 m) high. Through the years, however, earthquakes and volcanic activity changed the features of the mountains. Glaciers that moved through the area during the Ice Age further eroded—or wore away—the mountain peaks. Rain and wind continued to eat away at the mountains, leveling them to their current heights. The portion of the Appalachians that begins in central Pennsylvania and runs to the southwest is called the Allegheny Mountains. The Alleghenies include the highest point in Pennsylvania, Mount Davis, which stands 3,213 feet (979 m) high.

The Alleghenies give way to a series of smaller mountain ranges, including the Jacks, the Tuscarora, and the Blue mountains. These ranges are located in an area known as the Great Valley region. Harrisburg is located on the Susquehanna River in the Great Valley region. The city of Allentown, on the Lehigh River, is also in the Great Valley.

Moving eastward from the Alleghenies and the Great Valley region, the land flattens out. The land becomes level at the Piedmont Plateau. The Piedmont extends from Pennsylvania into New Jersey and Maryland, and it continues south toward Alabama. In Pennsylvania, the Piedmont Plateau is not as rugged

Motorists traveling in the Alleghenies on the Pennsylvania Turnpike go through the Allegheny Mountain Tunnel, which is more than 1 mile (1.6 km) long.

as the Appalachian Plateau. Instead, it is a landscape of rolling hills and fertile soil. Many of Pennsylvania's farms are located here.

The southeastern corner of the state is part of the Atlantic Coastal Plain, which stretches down the eastern edge of the United States from New York to Florida. Like the Great Lakes Plain, the Atlantic Coastal Plain is mostly very flat and very fertile. It is home to Philadelphia. The city lies on the Delaware River, which separates Pennsylvania from New Jersey.

Waterways

Pennsylvania is dotted with lakes. Some are natural lakes formed over many years of geologic change. Others are artificial lakes, created to keep Pennsylvania's rivers from flooding. Pennsylvania's largest natural lake is Conneaut Lake in the northwestern part of the state.

Located on the Delaware River, Philadelphia is the largest city in Pennsylvania and one of the largest in the United States.

This kayaker on the Susquehanna River is about to pass under the Rockville Bridge, near Harrisburg. At the time it was built in the early 1900s, the Rockville Bridge was the longest stone-arch railway bridge in the world.

Many rivers flow through the mountains, creating some of the most beautiful waterfalls on the East Coast. The rivers of Pennsylvania provided a major means of transportation for many years. Their usefulness was greatly increased by a series of human-made canals that were constructed as early as 1797. These canals bypassed rapids and falls, and they connected rivers. They allowed people and cargo to travel over rugged land features such as parts of the Alleghenies. Large floods have destroyed some canals, but historical markers point out where many of the canals were dug.

The Climate

Pennsylvania enjoys four distinct weather seasons. The average temperature in the winter is about 30 degrees Fahrenheit (−1 degree Celsius). Sometimes the temperature drops below 0 °F (−18 °C), especially in the mountains. The northern and western parts of Pennsylvania are usually colder in the winter than the southern and eastern portions of the state. Pennsylvania winters also bring snow and ice.

Pennsylvania has more historic covered bridges than any other U.S. state. Covering a bridge kept snow and ice off the roadway during Pennsylvania's cold winters.

In the spring, temperatures begin to warm up. This season can also include heavy rainfall. By June, summer temperatures usually rise to 60 °F to 80 °F (15 °C–27 °C). Besides high temperatures, the summer also brings humidity. The big cities, such as Philadelphia, can become the hottest places in July and August. But as fall approaches, temperatures tend to cool down quickly.

Wildlife

At one time, Pennsylvania was covered with forests. As European settlers came to the state, many trees were cut down to build houses, furniture, and wagons. The forests also supplied wood for fires to keep the settlers warm and to cook their food. As the population grew, more land was cleared to create farmland for crops and livestock. The lumber industry thrived in Pennsylvania during the 1800s and into the 1900s. By the early 1900s, several forests had been completely destroyed. Pennsylvania eventually began to take steps to restore its forests. Today, the state has nearly 17 million acres (6.9 million hectares) of woods, covering about 58 percent of its land area.

These forests are home to trees such as maple, oak, birch, pine, and elm. In the fall, Pennsylvania forests and hills turn lovely shades of orange, red, and yellow as the leaves change colors. Flowers bloom alongside the trees. Pennsylvania's state flower, the mountain laurel, grows wild in the forests, as do azaleas and rhododendrons.

Pennsylvania's forests and fields are also home to rabbits, raccoons, opossums, deer, squirrels, and bats. The white-tailed deer can be found nearly everywhere and is the official state animal. On a nature hike, visitors might also spot beavers, minks, woodchucks, and chipmunks. Black

Quick Facts

STATE CONSERVATION PLANT

The state of Pennsylvania has an official beautification and conservation plant: the hardy Penngift crownvetch. It features pink and white flowers and is often planted along roadsides and in other places not only for decoration but to help control erosion. It is also used for livestock feed.

Hikers in the Allegheny National Forest in northwestern Pennsylvania have a chance to see many kinds of plant and animal life.

bears and bobcats were once almost extinct in the state, but their numbers have increased.

The state is also home to many different types of birds. There are plenty of wild turkeys and ruffed grouse. Ducks, geese, and herons can be found feeding at the state's waterways. Robins, sparrows, larks, chickadees, owls, hawks, and falcons may be seen in the skies or perched in the trees.

Wild turkeys are a common sight in many areas of Pennsylvania.

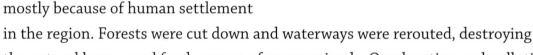

Endangered Wildlife in Pennsylvania

Many species—or types—of plants and animals that lived in the state hundreds or thousands of years ago are no longer around. This is mostly because of human settlement in the region. Forests were cut down and waterways were rerouted, destroying the natural homes and food sources of many animals. Overhunting and pollution have also affected certain animal species. They have become endangered—that is, in danger of dying out or disappearing from the state.

Some species have been saved from becoming extinct (dying out). Bald eagles used to fly across Pennsylvania skies and nest in the tall trees. But for most of the twentieth century, there were no bald eagles left in the state. Laws were passed restricting people from harming these eagles. Conservation efforts to breed and release these striking birds began. As a result, the population slowly began to increase. Today, you might see bald eagles living in watery areas in most of the state's counties. Elk are another example. These animals have twice become almost extinct in the Allegheny Mountains. But today, Pennsylvania has several hundred elk.

A number of species of plants and animals are still endangered in Pennsylvania. Among them are birds such as the short-eared owl, mammals such as the Delmarva fox squirrel, and some types of sturgeons, shiners, sunfish, and other fish.

Plants & Animals

Brook Trout

Brook trout can be found in Pennsylvania's cool lakes and streams. These trout are very colorful fish, with light-green backs highlighted with yellow and black spots. They are the only trout native to Pennsylvania streams. The brook trout is Pennsylvania's official state fish.

Great Blue Heron

The great blue heron is the largest member of the heron family in North America. This bird can be more than 3 feet (1 m) tall and is an excellent fisher. It catches its food by wading in shallow water, then waiting patiently without moving until a fish swims by. Once it sees a fish, it slowly folds its long neck back, then quickly plunges its head into the water and catches the fish with its long, sharp beak.

Firefly

On summer nights, most fields and forests in Pennsylvania are filled with the blinking lights of fireflies. Scientists believe that a firefly has two uses for its flashing light: to scare away creatures that might want to eat it and to attract a mate. A specific type of firefly—*Photuris pennsylvanica De Geer*—is the state's official insect.

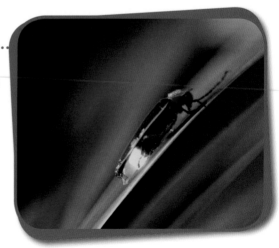

Striped Skunk

Striped skunks live in forests and near farmland. They eat insects, fruits, plants, and sometimes mice. Skunks are bushy tailed and black, with bold white stripes running down their backs. When frightened or threatened, these little creatures release a very strong scent that most animals—including humans—cannot stand.

Blackberries

Blackberry bushes grow wild in the mountainous regions of Pennsylvania. Their long branches are covered with thorns and create hedges of tangled brambles. These offer great hiding places for small forest creatures. In the spring, blackberry flowers bloom, and in the late summer, sweet berries grow on the branches.

Slippery Elm

Pennsylvania has more than one hundred different species of native trees, and slippery elm is one of them. Slippery elm can grow to be 60 feet (18 m) or more tall. The wood is sometimes used to make furniture. The inner bark of the tree has been used for many hundreds of years as a medicine. Americans Indians used elm bark to build canoes.

From the Beginning

Pennsylvania has a rich and interesting history, created by the different people who have lived in the region: American Indians; English, Dutch, Swedish, and German settlers; and many others. Their experiences and influences have shaped the state into what it is today.

Early Peoples

American Indians lived in what is now Pennsylvania for thousands of years before the first Europeans arrived. The first people to inhabit the area most likely lived in small tribes. They probably traveled from place to place, hunting and gathering food along the way. These people most likely moved with the seasons. In the summer, they might live near the rivers, where they could catch fish. In the fall, they might move toward the mountains, where they could eat wild berries, nuts, and other plants,

Quick Facts

WINDOW INTO PREHISTORIC TIMES

The Meadowcroft Rockshelter, located southwest of Pittsburgh, is one of North America's oldest archaeological sites. Archaeologists—scientists who study past human life and activities—have found plant and animal remains, as well as evidence that humans may have spent time near the shelter as early as 16,000 years ago.

These young Pennsylvanians pretend to be colonial soldiers during a reenactment of an American Revolution battle.

as well as hunt many types of animals. In the winter, they might hunt bigger animals that lived in the mountains.

As time passed, some of the tribes built more permanent villages, mostly along the major rivers. These people hunted animals in the nearby woods and planted crops on their land. There were several different American Indian groups living in the area when European settlers began arriving in the 1600s.

The Susquehannock, who lived along the Susquehanna River, were the first American Indians in the region to make contact with the new settlers. The Susquehannock were very interested in setting up trade with the Europeans. They traded animal hides and other goods for European supplies such as cloth and tools. By the end of the 1600s, though, there were only a few hundred Susquehannock left. Many died during wars with other American Indian groups. Others died from diseases brought by the European settlers.

The remaining members of the Susquehannock tribe moved farther west to lands along the Conestoga River. The Susquehannock who lived in this region

The Iroquois lived in large dwellings called longhouses.

were called the Conestoga. The Conestoga were craftspeople and farmers and lived peaceably with the neighboring colonists. But their numbers were few and continued to decrease as members of the tribe died or moved away. In 1763, all except two of the remaining Conestoga were killed by a group of angry white settlers. The settlers—known as the Paxton Boys—were angry with other American Indian groups, but they took their revenge on the Conestoga.

At the same time, American Indian tribes including the Iroquois, the Lenape (or Delaware), and the Shawnee lived in the region. The Lenape had occupied the area along the Delaware River in the eastern part of present-day Pennsylvania. They were pushed westward by European settlers and for a short time lived in the Alleghenies. After the American Revolution, they moved to Ohio. Today, most of their descendants live in Oklahoma. Little is recorded about the Shawnee who lived in the Pennsylvania area. Like other American Indian groups, they were driven off their land by Europeans. Many Shawnee eventually settled in what is now the state of Oklahoma.

The Europeans

Many historians believe that English captain John Smith was the first European to visit the region we call Pennsylvania. Smith is believed to have sailed up the Susquehanna River and met with the Susquehannock people in 1608. A year later, the Dutch government hired Henry Hudson to sail to North America in search of a water route to Asia. Hudson sailed into Delaware Bay and claimed the surrounding land on behalf of the Dutch. Other Dutch explorers soon came and set up trading posts there, but they did not construct permanent settlements.

In 1638, an expedition from Sweden arrived and claimed ownership of the region. They called the area Nya Sverige, which meant "New Sweden." Tinicum Island, in the Delaware River, was later named the capital of the Swedish territory. (Today the site is part of Pennsylvania. It is located southwest of present-day Philadelphia.) In 1654, the Swedes captured a Dutch fort in what is now Delaware, but Swedish control was short-lived. The following year, the Dutch reclaimed the entire region for their government.

Then, in 1664, the English decided that they wanted the land and claimed the same area for the Duke of York. The English gained and maintained control of the region. Nearly twenty years later, the English king, Charles II, gave William Penn a portion of that land. This portion later became Pennsylvania.

The Charter of Pennsylvania

William Penn was a Quaker—a member of a religious group called the Society of Friends. The Quakers were not treated well in England, and Penn wanted to establish a new colony where Quakers—and others—could live peacefully and worship as they pleased. He asked King Charles II to grant him land for this purpose west of the Delaware River. The king agreed, both because he owed money to Penn's father and because he wanted to honor the father's loyal service as an admiral. Charles signed the land grant in 1681. This grant, called the Charter of Pennsylvania, gave Penn the right to establish a colony

This illustration shows William Penn receiving the Charter of Pennsylvania from King Charles II of England.

in North America. The king named the colony Pennsylvania ("Penn's woods"), in honor of William Penn's father.

Penn, as proprietor, or governor, arrived in 1682. Together with other settlers, he organized the local government using a constitution that he called the Frame of Government. This document stated that people had a right to own land and to govern themselves. (Self-government was a new concept for most Europeans, since many European countries at that time were ruled by kings and queens.) Penn also helped plan the city of Philadelphia. He chose its name, which means "brotherly love" in Greek. The city was central to Pennsylvania society, and it grew to become the largest city in the American colonies.

In Their Own Words

Any government is free to the people under it ... where the laws rule, and the people are a party to those laws.

—From William Penn's Frame of Government, 1682

Colonial Wars

The population of Pennsylvania continued to grow, but most of the new settlers lived in what is now eastern Pennsylvania. Westward expansion was limited by the thick forests, the mountains, and a lack of roads wide enough to allow the passage of horse-drawn wagons. But some settlers did venture west in search of more land.

Both France and Britain wanted control of the land west of the established colonies, in spite of the fact that the area was already inhabited by American Indians. French and British newcomers started settlements there. Both countries built military forts in the region. This included land that is now

Quick Facts

FIRST WOMAN GOVERNOR
William Penn became very sick in 1712 and was no longer able to carry out his duties as proprietor, or governor, of Pennsylvania. His wife, Hannah, took over and ran the colony until her death in 1726.

George Washington (center) led the colonial and British forces who unsuccessfully tried to prevent French troops from capturing Fort Necessity during the French and Indian War.

part of western Pennsylvania. From 1689 to 1763, France and Britain fought over land rights in a series of four wars. As the tensions between the French and British grew, some American Indian groups took sides with one or the other country. In 1754, the French and Indian War—the last of the four wars—broke out. One of the first battles of this war was fought at Fort Necessity, near Farmington. There, the French and their Indian allies defeated a force of British and colonial men commanded by George Washington. It was the only time in his military career that Washington surrendered to an enemy. The site is now Fort Necessity National Battlefield. The French and Indian War lasted nine years. In the end, Britain won. As a result of the 1763 treaty ending the war, the British controlled land in Canada, a large amount of land between the colonies and the Mississippi River, and some land in what is now Florida.

Independence

By the mid–1700s, many colonists were unhappy with British control. They did not like Britain's taxes and trade rules. Many wanted the colonies to become independent and govern themselves. In 1774, representatives from most of the American colonies met in Philadelphia for the First Continental Congress. They decided that the colonies would no longer trade with Britain. By April 1775, the American Revolution had begun, and colonists were fighting the British. A month after the start of the war, the Second Continental Congress began meeting in Philadelphia. The following year, it voted for independence from Britain and issued the Declaration of Independence, which stated that the colonies deserved more rights and were no longer loyal to Britain.

This picture shows (left to right) Benjamin Franklin, Thomas Jefferson, John Adams, Robert Livingston, and Roger Sherman discussing the Declaration of Independence, which Jefferson had written.

Though colonial forces won some victories at the beginning of the war, the colonists' Continental Army faced many problems fighting the British. The British military men were well trained and had spent years fighting in or preparing to fight in battles. Most colonial soldiers were craftsmen or farmers or had held other nonmilitary jobs. Fighting and traveling from battle to battle was new to them. At first, these colonists did not have good weapons or the skills to use them. Over time, they grew stronger and more skilled, but battles against the British were still very difficult to win.

A few major battles in the American Revolution occurred in Pennsylvania. In September 1777, General George Washington and his men fought British troops at the Battle of Brandywine. Washington's men were forced to retreat. Later that month, the British soundly defeated a colonial force led by General Anthony Wayne in the Battle of Paoli near Philadelphia, and a few days after that, the British took over the city. Washington's forces again faced British troops near

Colonial troops face off against the British at the Battle of Brandywine in 1777.

Philadelphia at the Battle of Germantown in October. The British won the battle, and the colonial army had to retreat.

The following winter months were difficult for many colonial troops. Starting in mid-December, Washington and his men stayed in Valley Forge, located northwest of Philadelphia. His army was cold, tired, and hungry. The men did not have enough warm clothing, blankets, or food. During the winter at Valley Forge, many soldiers died from illness. Others deserted—or ran away from—the army.

In February 1778, conditions began to improve. More supplies were brought in. Baron Friedrich von Steuben, a military man from Prussia (an area largely in the present-day country of Germany), volunteered to help train Washington's men. By spring of that year, they had regained their strength and confidence, and they continued to fight British forces. With help from France, the colonial armies made progress against the British. The British forces left Philadelphia in June.

As the fighting continued, the British found allies among some American Indian tribes. In July 1778, some Iroquois in the region joined with the British to fight groups of settlers living in eastern Pennsylvania. The area, known as the Wyoming Valley, is near present-day Wilkes-Barre. A few hundred colonial troops and settlers

were killed during the Wyoming Valley Massacre, and many settlers fled. In turn, colonial forces later destroyed several Iroquois villages in the area.

The American Revolution officially ended in 1783, and the colonies became an independent nation, the United States of America. In Philadelphia, a national constitution was written in 1787, after much debate at the Constitutional Convention that met there from May to September. Then the colonies began to ratify, or approve, the document. Pennsylvania was the second state (after Delaware) to approve the Constitution, doing so on December 12, 1787. Philadelphia served as the capital of the new nation from 1790 to 1800, when the national government moved to Washington, D.C.

The 1800s

Pennsylvania continued to grow and prosper into the 1800s. Cities flourished, farms thrived, and industry expanded. Pennsylvania manufactured a large portion of the country's goods. Its steel mills, coal mines, and factories helped the economy. Pennsylvania was also well known for its glass production.

Pennsylvania's waterways were important for the transportation of people and goods. The state's first canal, the Conewago Canal, on the west bank of the Susquehanna River, was completed in 1797. About 1 mile (1.6 km) long, it allowed boats to bypass rocks and rapids in the Susquehanna and travel from York Haven to Columbia by water. More canal systems were established to improve travel and trade. In 1825, the Schuylkill Canal, actually a collection of

Locomotives such as this one were used on Pennsylvania's railroads in the first half of the 1800s.

separate canals and dam-created pools, became the first long canal project in Pennsylvania. By 1828, it measured 108 miles (174 km) in length, stretching from Port Carbon via Reading to Philadelphia, and it was used mainly to carry coal. Then, in 1834, the Pennsylvania Canal, which included a railroad segment that went up one side of the mountains and down the other, began enabling people and goods to more easily cross the Alleghenies. A series of large floods eventually destroyed many of the canals, but a few stretches of the Pennsylvania Canal have been preserved or restored. Railroads were expanded in the state in the 1850s, further improving Pennsylvania's transportation system.

In colonial times, many Pennsylvanians owned slaves. Slavery gradually disappeared in Pennsylvania after a law against it was adopted in 1780. The state became one of the many safe places for freed or escaped slaves to start new lives. The Underground Railroad was a network of people who helped African-American slaves from the South escape to freedom in the North and in Canada, where slavery was illegal. Some historians estimate that more than 100,000 people tried to leave the South through the Underground Railroad. Many escaping slaves died along the way. Others were caught and taken back to their masters. But many managed to make their way to freedom. The borough (a community similar to a town) of Columbia, along the Susquehanna River in Lancaster County, became a popular place for runaway slaves to settle.

The slavery issue was one of the reasons why the Civil War began in 1861. A total of eleven Southern states seceded—or separated—from the United States. They formed the Confederate States of America. Pennsylvania remained a part of the United States, which was also called the Union. The state sent more than 400,000 men to fight the Confederate forces. State residents provided supplies and food for the Union troops. Pennsylvania also produced much of the military equipment that was used.

Confederate and Union forces fought many bloody battles. One of the most famous was fought in Gettysburg, Pennsylvania, in 1863. The Battle of Gettysburg lasted from July 1 through July 3. About 50,000 soldiers were wounded or killed, making the battle one of the bloodiest in U.S. history. Gettysburg marked the northernmost point that any Confederate army reached. Defeated there, the Confederates were forced to retreat. President Abraham Lincoln delivered his famous Gettysburg Address on the battlefield in 1863. This short but eloquent

In Their Own Words

It is hereby enacted . . . That all Persons, as well Negroes, and Mulattos, as others, who shall be born within this State, from and after the Passing of this Act, shall not be deemed and considered as Servants for Life or Slaves; and that all Servitude for Life or Slavery of Children in Consequence of the Slavery of their Mothers, in the Case of all Children born within this State from and after the passing of this Act as aforesaid, shall be, and hereby is, utterly taken away, extinguished and for ever abolished.

—From An Act for
the Gradual Abolition
of Slavery, 1780

President Abraham Lincoln delivered his famous Gettysburg Address in 1863. The speech honored the Union soldiers who had fought at the Battle of Gettysburg, and it reminded people of the freedoms those soldiers were fighting to protect.

speech honored those who had fought and died for the country and its freedoms. The South eventually surrendered to the North in 1865, and the war ended. The Confederate states rejoined the United States, the Thirteenth Amendment to the U.S. Constitution ended slavery nationwide, and the country started rebuilding and reuniting.

Through the end of the 1800s, Pennsylvania's economy continued to thrive. In addition to mining, manufacturing, and farming, there was oil—the discovery of oil in the northwestern corner of the state marked the beginning of the American oil industry. Jobs were plentiful, and people from the war-torn Southern states, as well as immigrants from Scotland, Ireland, Russia, and Eastern Europe, came to Pennsylvania in hopes of making better lives. Work in the factories and mines, however, proved dangerous and did not provide as much money as the workers had expected. In the late 1800s, many of these workers demanded better pay and safer working conditions. Some of the first American labor unions were formed in Pennsylvania. These were groups of workers who banded together to demand better conditions and better pay.

The 1900s and Today

Pennsylvania continued to be one of the leading industrial states in the twentieth century. Unfortunately, in 1929 the Great Depression started, a severe downturn in the nation's economy that caused massive unemployment and hardship. Like many other states, Pennsylvania was hit hard. At one point, almost 80 percent of the workers at the state's steel mills and in its coal mines had lost their jobs. Since these were two of the biggest industries in Pennsylvania, the job losses meant that many people living in the state were unemployed. Without jobs, these workers had no money to feed their families or keep their homes. Most people could not afford to buy many products, so the merchants and farmers who provided these products to the public also suffered. Many people left the state to search for work elsewhere.

In 1931, unemployed miners organized a march in Washington, Pennsylvania, to seek government aid.

FIRST SUPERHIGHWAY

In 1940, the first section of the Pennsylvania Turnpike was completed. This section, 160 miles (257 km) long, was the country's first high-speed, multilane highway. The turnpike served as a model for most of the country's modern superhighways.

The state and national governments set up programs to help. Workers were employed by government to build and fix bridges, highways, and dams. Others were paid to work in the forests.

In 1939, World War II began in Europe. The United States joined the war in 1941. As in World War I, in which the United States fought from 1917 to 1918, the state sent many soldiers to serve in the military. Pennsylvania mines and factories also provided supplies for the war effort. Workers were hired to operate the steel mills, factories, and coal mines.

After the war, the state's economy prospered for a time, but then demand for Pennsylvania steel and coal declined, and many factories were shut down. It took many years, but the state's economy eventually bounced back. While mining and manufacturing continued to some extent, other areas of the economy, such as services, became more significant. New industries became important. Computers are one example. Pennsylvania played an important early role in their development. ENIAC, the first large-scale general-purpose electronic digital computer, was built in Philadelphia at the University of Pennsylvania in 1946. Also in Philadelphia, the Remington Rand Corporation made the first commercial computer, the Univac I, in 1951.

In part as a result of the state's reliance for many years on mining and manufacturing, Pennsylvania's environment suffered, and air and water pollution were serious problems. But in recent decades, the state's air and water have generally become cleaner. Partly this was a result of changes in the state's economy. But a very important factor was the passage of state and federal laws protecting the environment. The state has also taken action to preserve the many historic sites and landmarks that are part of the heritage of Pennsylvania.

Important Dates

★ **14,000 BCE** Early native peoples may already be living in the region that now includes Pennsylvania.

★ **1608** The English captain John Smith becomes the first white man to explore the Susquehanna River area.

★ **1638–1674** Dutch, Swedish, and English settlers establish the first permanent European settlements in the region.

★ **1682** William Penn establishes the colony of Pennsylvania.

★ **1754–1763** Britain and France fight the French and Indian War. As a result of its victory, Britain gains undisputed control of almost all the land east of the Mississippi River.

★ **1776** The Declaration of Independence is adopted in Philadelphia.

★ **1783** The colonists win the American Revolution.

★ **1787** Pennsylvania becomes the second state to ratify the new U.S. Constitution, written at the Constitutional Convention in Philadelphia.

★ **1790–1800** Philadelphia serves as the capital of the United States.

★ **1812** Harrisburg becomes the state capital.

★ **1863** Union forces defeat the Confederates in the Battle of Gettysburg during the Civil War.

★ **1889** A massive flood, caused by failure of a dam, kills more than 2,200 people in the Johnstown area.

★ **1940** The first section of the Pennsylvania Turnpike opens.

★ **1957** The first U.S. full-scale nuclear power plant goes into service in Shippingport.

★ **1979** An accident at the Three Mile Island nuclear power plant causes widespread concern.

★ **2001** United Airlines Flight 93, hijacked by terrorists, crashes in a field near Somerset on September 11.

★ **2008** Comcast Center in Philadelphia is completed. With a height of 975 feet (297 m), it is the tallest building in Pennsylvania and the fourteenth-tallest in the United States.

The People

In 1790, when the first census, or count, of all the people in the United States was taken, the population of Pennsylvania was almost 435,000. Sixty years later, the number of people living in Pennsylvania had dramatically increased, to more than 2 million. The number of residents continued to grow rapidly. In 2007, the U.S. Census Bureau estimated that Pennsylvania had a population of more than 12.4 million people. The bureau also reported that the people of Pennsylvania come from a wide variety of cultures.

The First Residents

American Indians hunted, farmed, and lived for centuries on the land that is now Pennsylvania. Major groups in the region when the first Europeans arrived included the Iroquois, Susquehannock, Shawnee, and Lenape. Loss of land and hunting grounds, European settlement, and diseases brought by the Europeans decreased the Indian population in the region.

The U.S. Census Bureau estimated that in 2007, American Indians accounted for only about 0.1 percent of the state's population. Today, there are no federally recognized Indian reservations in Pennsylvania. But many American Indians from different tribes and nations live in the state. American Indians in Pennsylvania own farms, have jobs in towns and cities, and hold office in local and state governments. Throughout the year, festivals and powwows (American

This person in traditional dress dances at a powwow in Sullivan County.

This photograph of a group of Iroquois was taken around 1900.

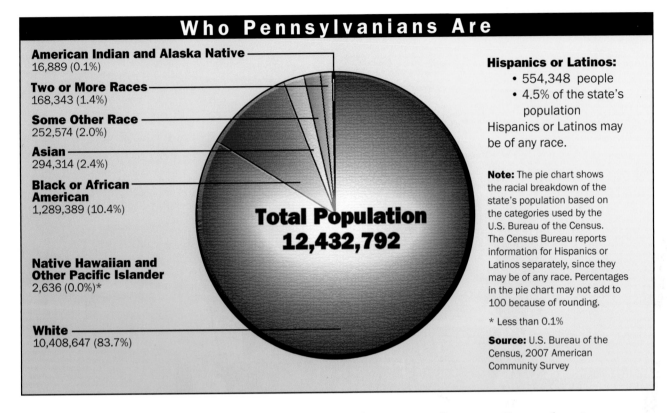

Who Pennsylvanians Are

American Indian and Alaska Native
16,889 (0.1%)

Two or More Races
168,343 (1.4%)

Some Other Race
252,574 (2.0%)

Asian
294,314 (2.4%)

Black or African American
1,289,389 (10.4%)

Native Hawaiian and Other Pacific Islander
2,636 (0.0%)*

White
10,408,647 (83.7%)

Total Population 12,432,792

Hispanics or Latinos:
• 554,348 people
• 4.5% of the state's population

Hispanics or Latinos may be of any race.

Note: The pie chart shows the racial breakdown of the state's population based on the categories used by the U.S. Bureau of the Census. The Census Bureau reports information for Hispanics or Latinos separately, since they may be of any race. Percentages in the pie chart may not add to 100 because of rounding.

* Less than 0.1%

Source: U.S. Bureau of the Census, 2007 American Community Survey

Indian fairs, with dancing and more) take place across the state. Pennsylvania also has many American Indian historical landmarks and museums.

The Pennsylvania Dutch

The people known as the Pennsylvania Dutch are descendants of European immigrants who spoke a form of German ("Deutsch"). They are not descendants of Dutch people from Holland. Their ancestors began coming to Pennsylvania in the seventeenth century. Many wanted to get away from wars in Europe and find religious freedom in a new land. By 1775, the Pennsylvania Dutch made up one-third of the colony's population. Today, a large proportion of the Pennsylvania Dutch live in the Lancaster area, where they are estimated to number close to 100,000 people. Many of them belong to such Christian sects, or groups, as the Amish, Mennonites, and Brethren.

Some Pennsylvania Dutch live in much the same way as their ancestors. They do not believe in modern conveniences such as electricity, telephones, or cars.

Many Amish people and some other Pennsylvania Dutch drive from place to place in horse-drawn carriages, just as their ancestors did.

They run their farms in nearly the same manner as their ancestors did centuries ago. On some roads in Lancaster County, Pennsylvania Dutch horse-drawn carriages can be seen alongside cars. But not all Pennsylvania Dutch live in seventeenth- or eighteenth-century conditions. Some people of Pennsylvania Dutch descent use all types of modern technology and conveniences.

A Mix of Cultures

According to the U.S. Census Bureau, as of 2007, Pennsylvania's population was about 84 percent Caucasian—or white. Most of these people are of European heritage. Some are descended from the earliest European settlers: the Dutch, the Swedish, and the English. Other white residents can trace their ancestors to the German, Polish, Italian, Irish, Scottish, and other immigrants who came to the state over the centuries. New European immigrants, as well as Americans with European backgrounds who relocate from other states, continue to move into Pennsylvania and make it their home.

Today, African Americans make up the largest minority group in the state. Approximately a tenth of the population is African American. Between 1780 and 1847, slavery was gradually ended in Pennsylvania. Many freed slaves chose to live in and around Philadelphia and other Pennsylvania cities. Many of their descendants make Pennsylvania their home today. In the twentieth century, many African Americans from the South settled in the state. This was especially true in the years after World Wars I and II. Many factory and other industrial jobs were available in Pennsylvania at that time, and workers in these jobs tended to earn more money than, say, people who worked on farms in the South.

PAINTING A PENNSYLVANIA DUTCH TILE

Many Pennsylvania Dutch brought colorful good luck signs—sometimes called hex signs—to their new homes. They believed that special symbols such as birds, hearts, stars, flowers, and fruits brought good luck. Colors also had meaning—red for love, blue for truth, yellow for life, and green for good fortune and happiness.

WHAT YOU NEED

1 piece of light cardboard (an empty cereal box or the back of a writing pad)

Newspaper

Scotch tape

1 white ceramic tile—4 inches by 4 inches, or 10 cm by 10 cm (found in hardware stores)

Glass and tile paint (found at craft stores) in red, blue, and yellow

Paintbrushes

1 sheet of felt (at least 8 inches by 11 inches, or 20 cm by 28 cm)

Craft or tacky glue

To make the stencil:

Draw your design on the cardboard. You can draw a simple bird, a pineapple, hearts, flowers, or a combination of some or all of these. Make sure that your design will fit on the tile. Cut out the design. Ask an adult to help if the cardboard is too hard to cut. Throw away the cutouts and keep the sheet of cardboard with the open spaces (your stencil).

To paint the tile:

Spread newspaper to protect your work surface. Tape the cardboard stencil to the tile. Brush different colors of paint over the different holes in the cardboard. (You can combine the yellow and blue paint to make green paint.) Paint the lighter colors first, then the darker ones. If you make a mistake, you can wipe the wet paint off with a damp piece of paper towel. When you are done painting, keep your stencil taped to the tile and allow the tile to dry for about half an hour.

Make sure the paint is dry before lifting the stencil. If you find a mistake after you have removed the stencil, you can gently scratch the unwanted paint off with your fingernail.

Let the tile air-dry for several hours.

When the tile is dry, cut a piece of felt and glue it to the back of the tile. You can use the tile as a paperweight or coaster or as a decorative piece for your home.

Hispanic and Asian Pennsylvanians

More than half a million Hispanic people live in Pennsylvania. Hispanics started moving to the state in the nineteenth century. Some came as experienced farmers and found work in agriculture. Others found jobs in different lines of work, and many opened their own businesses. Many came from Puerto Rico. In recent years, the Hispanic population has grown rapidly to include people from Mexico, Cuba, the Dominican Republic, and other countries. In many of Pennsylvania's cities, you can find businesses, restaurants, and stores owned by Hispanic Americans. Throughout the year in different parts of Pennsylvania, residents hold festivals and other events celebrating Hispanic culture.

Asian Americans make up a little more than 2 percent of the state's population. The state's Asian population includes people of Indian, Chinese, Filipino, Vietnamese, Korean, and Japanese heritage. Some of these people are the children or grandchildren of immigrants who came to the state many years ago. Others are new residents. Regardless of how long they have lived in the state, their influence can be seen in different parts of Pennsylvania.

Philadelphia has a thriving Chinatown. This part of the city first attracted Chinese immigrants who arrived more than one hundred years ago. Through the years, visitors and residents have enjoyed—and continue to enjoy—Chinatown's shops, restaurants, and cultural celebrations.

Celebrating Traditions

Historically, Pennsylvania has always been known as a place where people from many different backgrounds and cultures gathered. Through the years, the racial and ethnic makeup of Pennsylvania's people has changed. But this diversity has helped make Pennsylvania into the appealing state that it is today.

Some of Pennsylvania's best-known traditions have their roots in the state's immigrant heritage. Philadelphia's highly popular Mummers' Parade is one example. Held every year on January 1, the parade features bands and other marchers in fancy and colorful costumes. The origins of this event go back to the customs of the region's early Swedish settlers, who would celebrate the New Year

Pennsylvania children study their state's history and learn about their various cultural traditions.

Philadelphia's Mummers' Parade, held every New Year's Day, features almost two dozen bands in colorful costumes.

Groups of visitors arrive at the National Shrine of Our Lady of Czestochowa in Doylestown. The shrine is the site of an annual Polish-American festival.

by dressing up in elaborate costumes and walking through the streets ringing bells and visiting friends. By the beginning of the twentieth century, this practice had evolved into an organized parade. Today, more than forty social clubs in the Philadelphia area provide the parade's thousands of marchers, and tens of thousands of people line the parade route to enjoy the show.

Pennsylvanians of various ethnic backgrounds enjoy celebrating their heritage. Irish Americans and others turn out for the annual St. Patrick's Day parades in Philadelphia, Pittsburgh, and other cities around the state. Philadelphia's Columbus Day parade honors the heritage of the area's Italian Americans. An annual Polish-American festival is held at the National Shrine of Our Lady of Czestochowa in Doylestown.

Benjamin Franklin: Statesman and Scientist

Franklin was born in Boston in 1706 but moved to Philadelphia when he was seventeen. Despite having only two years of formal education, Franklin became a printer, author, inventor, scientist, educator, politician, and diplomat. He is well known for using a kite to prove that lightning and electricity are related. Franklin is called one of the Founding Fathers of the United States because he had an important role in drafting the Declaration of Independence and the Constitution.

James Buchanan: United States President

Buchanan, the fifteenth president of the United States, was born in 1791 in Franklin County. His family lived in a log cabin at a frontier outpost in Cove Gap but later moved to Mercersburg. Before becoming president, Buchanan was a U.S. congressman and senator. He also served as a minister to Russia and Great Britain (which means he handled foreign affairs between the United States and these countries), as ambassador to Great Britain, and as secretary of state under President James K. Polk. Buchanan was president from 1857 to 1861.

Rachel Carson: Environmentalist

Carson was born in 1907 on a farm near Springdale. Throughout her youth, she was curious about nature. Carson was a very good writer and published her first magazine piece, a story, when she was in the fourth grade. Carson's main concerns were studying, preserving, and protecting the environment—and sharing her findings with the public. One of her books, *Silent Spring*, pointed out the health dangers of pesticides. She was one of the first people to call attention to how those chemicals pollute the land and water.

Bill Cosby: Actor and Comedian

Cosby was born in Philadelphia in 1937. As a comedian and actor who is African American, he has been able to overcome prejudice and bring attention to the similarities—rather than the differences—among people of different backgrounds. Cosby has starred in many television shows for adults and children. In 1998, he was honored at the Kennedy Center in Washington, D.C., for a lifetime of achievement in the arts.

Kobe Bryant: Basketball Player

The son of a former professional basketball player, Bryant was born in Philadelphia in 1978. After starring in high school basketball, he joined the Los Angeles Lakers, a National Basketball Association team. He helped the Lakers win the league championship in 2000, 2001, 2002, and 2009, and he was named the league's Most Valuable Player in 2008.

Tara Lipinski: Figure Skater

Born in Philadelphia in 1982, Lipinski started roller skating at the age of three and first tried ice skating when she was six. Lipinski became famous for performing difficult triple-loop jumps on the ice. At the age of fourteen, she became the youngest person to win the world figure-skating championship. In 1998, at the age of fifteen, she was the youngest person to win an Olympic gold medal in figure skating.

Calendar of Events

★ **Mummers' Parade**

On the first day of January, Philadelphia holds its internationally famous Mummers' Parade. This is a celebration of clowns, fancy costumes, dancing, and music. "String" bands provide the music, but everyone—including the crowd—is invited to do the Mummers' Strut, a comical squat-kneed dance.

★ **Groundhog Day**

On February 2, people flock to Punxsutawney to learn how long winter will continue. Tradition says that if Punxsutawney Phil, the event's official groundhog, comes out of his hole and sees his shadow, you can expect six more weeks of winter. If he sees no shadow, then spring is around the corner.

★ **Maple Syrup Festival**

This festival is held in March in Erie's Asbury Woods. Visitors learn about making syrup, from the tapping of the trees to the boiling of the sap. Afterward, many enjoy a hearty breakfast of pancakes topped with freshly made pure maple syrup.

★ **Devon Horse Show and Country Fair**

This May event is the largest show of multibreed horses in the United States. Located outside Philadelphia, the fair offers a chance to watch children and adults run and jump their horses through a challenging course.

★ **Elfreth's Alley Fete Day**

Elfreth's Alley in Philadelphia claims to be one of the oldest residential streets in the United States. During this colonial festival in June, people can walk through the historic houses and be greeted by people dressed in colonial costumes.

★ Gettysburg Civil War Heritage Days

Over the course of a few days, visitors can see reenactments of the Battle of Gettysburg. Historians discuss the battle and the Civil War. The event, which usually begins at the end of June and extends into early July, also has a fireworks display and other entertainment.

★ Little League World Series

Williamsport is the birthplace of Little League Baseball, which began in 1939. Every August, the Little League World Series is held in neighboring South Williamsport, which also has a Little League museum.

★ Mushroom Festival

Southern Chester County grows more mushrooms than any other area in the United States. Every September, a big mushroom festival takes place on the first weekend after Labor Day at Kennett Square, also known as the Mushroom Capital of the World.

★ Native American Autumnal Festival in Airville

Every September, this popular festival is held at the Indian Steps Museum in Airville, west of Philadelphia. The museum has one of Pennsylvania's largest collections of American Indian artifacts, including arrowheads and tomahawks. One of the festival's highlights is a powwow.

How the Government Works

Pennsylvania is one of four U.S. states that are officially called commonwealths. (The other three commonwealths are Kentucky, Massachusetts, and Virginia.) The word *commonwealth* reflects the state's concern for the well-being of all its citizens. The word can mean a group of people (for example, all Pennsylvanians) who join together to promote their common good. Commonwealth or state, Pennsylvania has a system of state and local government units that help keep the state running.

Pennsylvania is represented in the U.S. Congress in Washington, D.C. Like all states, Pennsylvania has two members in the U.S. Senate. The number of members each state has in the U.S. House of Representatives is related to the state's population and can change after each U.S. census is taken. As of 2010, Pennsylvania had nineteen representatives in the U.S. House.

Local Government

The state is divided into sixty-seven counties. A county is made up of several cities or smaller communities, which are called boroughs or townships. Each county has its own government, usually run by commissioners. These commissioners handle issues that affect the many communities within the county. But each city, borough, or township also has its own local government. Local officials are elected by the residents of the community. Most cities and

Pennsylvania's legislature holds its meetings at the State Capitol in Harrisburg.

Branches of Government

EXECUTIVE ★ ★ ★ ★ ★ ★ ★ ★

The governor is the head of the executive branch. He or she is elected to a four-year term and cannot serve more than two terms in a row. The governor's responsibilities include approving or vetoing (rejecting) proposed laws and supervising the state budget. The executive branch also includes officials who work with the governor, such as the lieutenant governor, attorney general, and state treasurer.

LEGISLATIVE ★ ★ ★ ★ ★ ★ ★ ★

The legislative—or lawmaking—branch is the general assembly. Two houses make up the general assembly: the senate and the house of representatives. Senators serve four-year terms, and representatives serve for two years. There are 50 senators in the general assembly and 203 representatives.

JUDICIAL ★ ★ ★ ★ ★ ★ ★ ★

The judicial branch is responsible for making sure that laws are followed. The state supreme court heads this branch. This court has seven justices, who are elected to ten-year terms. Lower courts include the appellate courts (the superior court and the commonwealth court), the courts of common pleas, and the community courts. These courts are often limited to certain types of cases, based on the kind of crime or other matter involved.

boroughs are run by a mayor and a council, or group of officials. Townships are managed by commissioners or by supervisors. City, borough, and township governments are designed to address local problems. Such issues as local budgets and land use are managed by these units of governments. The public school system is managed by separate units of government called school districts.

Many Pennsylvania residents are active in local government. Some serve as officials. Many attend numerous meetings and hearings that address local problems. Through elections, in which they choose public officials and decide important issues, local residents are able to control how their community is run.

State Government

The state government is responsible for issues that affect the state as a whole.

Philadelphia's City Hall, with a statue of Benjamin Franklin at the top, is one of the city's most famous buildings. For many years after it was completed in 1901, the building was the tallest in Philadelphia.

The job of state officials includes drafting, approving, and enforcing laws; managing state budgets; and handling issues between Pennsylvania and other states and between Pennsylvania and the federal government in Washington, D.C. The center of the state government is Harrisburg, the state capital since the early nineteenth century.

Pennsylvania's state government is divided into three branches, which have different roles to play in governing the state. The executive branch is headed by the governor: the state's chief executive, or chief manager. The legislative branch passes laws for the state. The judicial branch includes the state's courts, which apply the laws to specific cases and may also decide whether a state law agrees with or violates the state constitution.

The Pennsylvania constitution describes the structure of the state

Quick Facts

CAPITALS
Tinicum Island (beginning in 1643), Chester (1682), Philadephia (1683), and Lancaster (1799) served as Pennsylvania's capitals before Harrisburg became the state capital in 1812.

Pennsylvania's house of representatives meets in this chamber within the State Capitol.

This photo shows the inside of the magnificent dome atop the State Capitol.

government and the powers of each branch of government. The state constitution also sets limits on the powers of government. This protects the rights of individuals. Pennsylvania has changed its constitution several times in the course of the state's history. The current constitution was adopted in 1968.

How a Bill Becomes a Law

The ideas behind new laws can come from different places—sometimes from legislators and sometimes from state residents. A state resident with an idea for a law can present it to his or her state representative or senator. A proposed law is called a bill. It takes only one senator or representative to help develop a proposal into a bill. But if more than one general assembly member supports the bill, chances are greater that it will become a law. It is also helpful if citizens are made aware of the bill. Then they can ask their assembly members to support it. Bills can cover a variety of topics. For example, one bill might increase taxes to help pay for road repairs. Another bill might require harsh punishments for people who commit very serious crimes. Other bills define people's jobs, such as the role of volunteer firefighters.

The state senator or representative originating a bill first takes it to the Legislative Reference Bureau. The bureau writes it in official legal language, making the bill ready for formal presentation. The bill is then given a name and number. It is first presented in the house where it originated. This means that if a state representative helped draft the bill, it is first presented in the house of representatives. If the bill came from a senator, then the presentation starts in the senate. The bill is introduced and then sent to a committee within the house or senate. The committee carefully studies the bill. Its job is to decide whether the bill should go to the whole house or senate to be voted on. The committee members base their decisions partly on public opinion. They may hold hearings to see how the public feels about the bill. If the committee finds that the public likes some of the ideas contained in the bill but not other parts of it, then

changes—or amendments—can be made. Ultimately, the committee may decide not to send the bill to all the members of the general assembly. When a bill is rejected by the committee considering it, it is said that the bill has "died in committee."

However, if the committee concludes that the bill is worthy, it will send the bill to the entire house or senate for further consideration. At this time, representatives or senators debate the merits of the bill and have a chance to change the bill by suggesting amendments. They then vote on the bill. If the bill is passed by a majority vote, it moves on to the other half of the general assembly. There, the same process is carried out. If both houses can agree on the final bill and any amendments that were made, it is passed to the governor.

The governor reviews the bill and must decide whether to approve it or veto it. If he or she approves, it becomes law. A bill that is vetoed by the governor can still become a law. For that to happen, the bill must be passed again by a two-thirds majority of each house of the general assembly.

The state encourages its residents to take an active part in their government. Many hearings are open to the public. Pennsylvanians can voice their concerns and give suggestions to their state legislators. Many legislators invite their constituents—that is, the residents they represent—to visit them at the State Capitol to learn more about the state government and its processes.

Making a Living

Agriculture, mining, manufacturing, and service industries help keep Pennsylvania's economy running. They supply goods and services used around the the world, and they provide jobs for millions of people in Pennsylvania.

Forests and Farms

Agriculture and other industries relying on natural resources have always played a large part in Pennsylvania's economy. The lumber industry was important during the eighteenth and nineteenth centuries. Millions of trees were harvested for lumber and for papermaking. As a result, Pennsylvania lost most of its forests. Today, much of the state is again covered by trees, and the forest-products industry again plays an important role. But instead of the pine and hemlock trees that once covered the land, hardwoods such as black cherry, oak, maple, walnut, poplar, and ash now predominate. Pennsylvania is the country's leading hardwood producer, accounting for about a tenth of total U.S. output. Pennsylvania also has many Christmas tree farms, which grow pine trees for the holidays.

Unlike the lumber industry, Pennsylvania's farming industry has remained relatively steady through the centuries, although the area devoted to farming has tended to decrease in recent decades. Today, about one-fourth of Pennsylvania

A girl enjoys a walk with her pony on a rural farm. About a quarter of the land in Pennsylvania is used for farming.

is farmland. Pennsylvania farmers harvest wheat, oats, mushrooms, soybeans, potatoes, and corn. Many acres are dedicated to apple orchards. Farmers in the southern part of the state grow tomatoes, grapes, peaches, and strawberries. Pennsylvania also produces cut flowers, shrubs, and ornamental trees for use across the country.

Animals raised in the state include hogs, sheep, and poultry. On many eastern and southeastern Pennsylvania fields, you might find herds of beef cattle grazing. Cows are also important to the dairy industry. Milk and other dairy products made up Pennsylvania's top-selling category of agricultural commodities in 2007. Poultry and eggs made up the second-largest category. Some Pennsylvania farmers raise llamas. Their hair can be used for clothing, and they can be trained to guard sheep herds.

Dairy farming is an important part of Pennsylvania's economy.

RECIPE FOR APPLESAUCE COOKIES

To make these tasty treats, you can use store-bought applesauce or make your own. Have an adult help you with the cutting and the cooking.

WHAT YOU NEED

$1\frac{1}{2}$ cups (375 milliliters) applesauce*

1 egg

$\frac{3}{4}$ cup (150 grams) sugar

1 teaspoon (5 g) cinnamon

1 teaspoon (5 g) baking soda

2 cups (240 g) all-purpose flour

$\frac{1}{2}$ cup (95 g) softened margarine

1 teaspoon (5 g) baking powder

Have an adult help you preheat the oven to 350 °F (175 °C). While the oven is heating, combine all the ingredients together and mix well. Drop small spoonfuls of the batter onto a greased cookie sheet. Bake the cookies for about 15 minutes or until they are a golden-brown color. When they are done, carefully remove the cookies and place them on a cooling rack. Be very careful because they will be hot. Once the cookies are cool, grab a glass of milk and dig in!

  *To make your own applesauce, have an adult help you with the following steps. Peel, core, and thinly slice six medium apples. Place the apple slices in a pan with 1 cup (250 ml) of water. Simmer the mixture for about 15 minutes and stir in 1/4 cup (50 g) sugar and a few sprinkles of cinnamon. Take the applesauce off the stove and let it cool. Once it is cool, you can eat it straight from a bowl or use it for your cookies.

Workers & Industries

Industry	Number of People Working in That Industry	Percentage of All Workers Who Are Working in That Industry
Education and health care	1,423,859	24.1%
Wholesale and retail businesses	872,543	14.7%
Manufacturing	785,551	13.3%
Publishing, media, entertainment, hotels, and restaurants	594,814	10.1%
Professionals, scientists, and managers	556,065	9.4%
Banking and finance, insurance, and real estate	389,771	6.6%
Construction	381,492	6.4%
Transportation and public utilities	321,985	5.4%
Other services	281,297	4.8%
Government	238,079	4.0%
Farming, fishing, forestry, and mining	70,835	1.2%
Totals	**5,916,291**	**100%**

Notes: Figures above do not include people in the armed forces. "Professionals" includes people such as doctors and lawyers. Percentages may not add to 100 because of rounding.

Source: U.S. Bureau of the Census, 2007 estimates

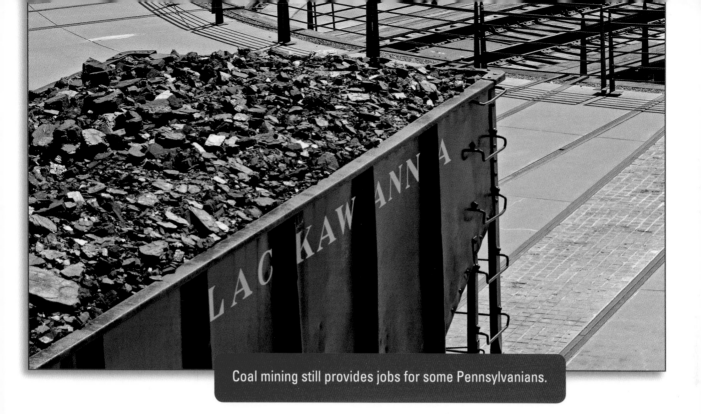

Coal mining still provides jobs for some Pennsylvanians.

Mining

Mined products include limestone, used for cement and other construction products. Many construction companies also use sand and gravel from the state. Pennsylvania coal is used for processing iron ore, heating homes, and generating electricity at power plants. In 1859, the first U.S. oil well was dug in Titusville. Small amounts of oil continue to be produced in the western part of the state, along with substantial amounts of natural gas.

Manufacturing

Pennsylvania's factories manufacture goods such as chemicals (including medicines),

World-famous Harley-Davidson motorcycles are manufactured in York, Pennsylvania.

food products, computer and electronic products, tools, and paper. The milk from the state's dairy farms is processed and made into a variety of foods. Pennsylvania food-processing plants make cookies, cakes, crackers, bread, and other treats. The state's snack food and candy industry accounts for more than $5 billion in sales a year.

A century ago, Pennsylvania was the top steel producer in the United States. Its steel was used in railroad tracks throughout the country. The framework for many skyscrapers and other buildings came from Pennsylvania's steel mills.

Much of the steel industry was centered in Pittsburgh, which was often called Smoky City because of its factories. Pennsylvania continues to make steel, although it no longer leads the country. In 2008, it accounted for about 6 percent of U.S. raw steel production.

In Their Own Words

The city has always its pillar of cloud by day and pillar of fire by night. A yellow haze hangs over the region. . . . Floating rivers of dense black smoke flow from hundreds of chimneys and flood the streets between the skyscrapers.

—Herbert Newton Casson describing Pittsburgh a century ago in his book *The Romance of Steel* (1907)

Quick Facts

ANDREW CARNEGIE AND CARNEGIE STEEL

Andrew Carnegie came to the United States from Scotland with his family in the 1840s, when he was twelve, and the family settled in the Pittsburgh area. As a young man, Carnegie worked for the Pennsylvania Railroad, where he was promoted to increasingly important positions. He also invested money in other industrial companies. In the 1870s and 1880s, he started or purchased several steel mills, which he combined into the Carnegie Steel Company. There was an increasing need for steel at that time for buildings and industrial equipment. Carnegie Steel became one of the largest steel manufacturers in the country, and Andrew Carnegie became one of the richest Americans of his time. The company did not always treat its workers well. In 1892, when workers at Carnegie's Homestead mill went on strike to protest a wage cut, the strike was broken up with the aid of armed guards, and several people were killed in a fight between guards and strikers. After he sold Carnegie Steel (for almost $500 million) in 1901, Carnegie donated hundreds of millions of dollars, largely to help establish numerous libraries, research centers, and colleges—including part of what is now Carnegie Mellon University in Pittsburgh.

Products & Resources

Mushrooms

Pennsylvania is the top mushroom-producing state. More than 800 million pounds (360 million kilograms) of mushrooms are produced in the United States each year. Pennsylvania accounts for well over half of that total.

Coal

Pennsylvania still ranks fourth in the United States for coal production. Mining, however, can damage the environment, and it can also be a dangerous way to make a living. Many laws have been passed to make coal mining a cleaner and safer industry.

Transportation

Since colonial times, transportation has been important to Pennsylvania. The state's location along major waterways helped—and still helps—the shipment of goods. The creation of canals and railroads further increased traffic through the state. Today, the state is home to major shipping ports and two major international airports.

Chemicals

Chemical manufacturing is one of Pennsylvania's major industries. Especially important is the manufacture of drugs, or pharmaceuticals. The state accounts for more than a tenth of U.S. pharmaceutical output. Other chemicals produced include those used in paints and glues.

Dairy Products

Pennsylvania is the fourth-highest producer of milk, ice cream, and butter in the country. Milk is the official state beverage.

Poultry

The state makes more than $1 billion a year from its poultry industry. Pennsylvania poultry products include eggs, turkeys, and chickens. Farms across the state raise and sell these products.

Services

Service industries include banking, health care, education, retail stores, restaurants, hotels, and government. More than three-fourths of workers in Pennsylvania are employed in such industries.

Tourism is an important part of the state's economy. Millions of visitors come to Pennsylvania every year. They spend money on hotels, restaurants, and souvenirs. The tourist industry employs hundreds of thousands of Pennsylvanians.

Historic Pennsylvania draws tourists of all ages. Many travel to Philadelphia to see its colonial sites. Some sites, such as the Liberty Bell and Independence Hall (where the Declaration of Independence was approved and the Constitution was written), are located downtown in Independence National Historical Park. Civil War enthusiasts often visit Gettysburg. One of the worst disasters in U.S. history is the focus of the Johnstown Flood National Memorial at St. Michael and the Flood Museum in Johnstown. Pennsylvania's rich railroad history is highlighted at places such as Scranton's Steamtown National Historic Site, which has one of the biggest collections of historic locomotives and rail cars in the United States.

Pennsylvania is home to many other museums and historical centers. Some of the best known are located in Philadelphia. These include the Franklin Institute (devoted to science), the Insectarium (for insect lovers), and the Philadelphia Museum of Art. Valley Forge National Historical Park is not far from Philadelphia. Pittsburgh also

Quick Facts

THE LIBERTY BELL
This famous bell, on display in Philadelphia, was ordered from England in 1752 to be hung in the building now called Independence Hall. The bell cracked and, in 1753, was twice melted down and recast. In the following years, it was rung to announce many important events. A major new crack developed in 1846 when it was rung for George Washington's birthday.

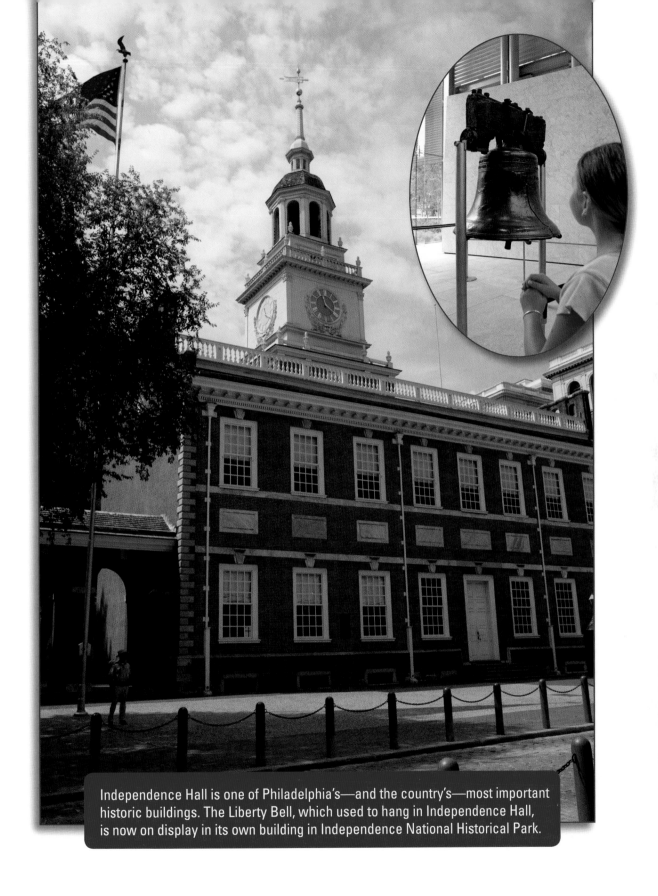

Independence Hall is one of Philadelphia's—and the country's—most important historic buildings. The Liberty Bell, which used to hang in Independence Hall, is now on display in its own building in Independence National Historical Park.

A visitor watches candy being made at the Hershey chocolate factory.

has several popular and well-respected museums, including the Carnegie Museum of Natural History, the Carnegie Museum of Art, the Carnegie Science Center, the Frick Art and Historical Center, and the Fort Pitt Museum.

Pennsylvania's famed snack food industry is concentrated in the southeastern part of the state. Lovers of chips and pretzels are drawn to the many factory tours in York and Lancaster counties. The world's largest chocolate factory is located in Hershey. The Hershey Company dates its origin to 1894, when Milton Hershey, its founder, opened a candy plant in Lancaster. Tourists come to Hershey to learn about and sample the company's sweet treats. Visitors also spend time at the Hershey theme park, garden, wildlife park, and spa.

A girl and her father enjoy trout fishing in Pennsylvania's Neshannock Creek.

Professional sports are popular—and big business—in the state. Many Major League Baseball fans in Pennsylvania root for the Philadelphia Phillies or the Pittsburgh Pirates. When football season arrives, fans cheer for the Pittsburgh Steelers or the Philadelphia Eagles of the National Football League. In the National Hockey League, the Philadelphia Flyers and Pittsburgh Penguins skate for Pennsylvania's two largest cities. In professional basketball, the state has the Philadelphia 76ers of the National Basketball Association.

People are also drawn to Pennsylvania's wilderness. With more than 2.1 million acres of state forests, the Allegheny National Forest, and more

The Delaware Water Gap National Recreation Area offers many opportunities for outdoor fun in a spectacularly beautiful setting.

than one hundred state parks, Pennsylvania is a haven for people who want to enjoy nature. Many families spend vacations amid the woods of the Poconos. The Delaware Water Gap National Recreation Area gets many visitors—particularly in the warm-weather months. The National Recreation Area spans a forty-mile stretch of the Delaware River, along the border of Pennsylvania and New Jersey. Visitors can enjoy swimming, fishing, canoeing, kayaking, and rafting, as well as hiking in the hills alongside the river.

State Flag & Seal

Pennsylvania's state coat of arms is represented on the state flag. On each side of the coat of arms is a horse rearing up on its hind legs. An eagle sits above with its wings wide open. The state motto—"Virtue, Liberty, and Independence"—is beneath the coat of arms. In the center of the coat of arms are the same three symbols present on the state seal: a ship, a plow, and three sheaves of wheat. Below them are a crossed cornstalk and olive branch. Pennsylvania's state flag was officially adopted in 1799.

Pennsylvania's state seal was made official in 1791. The front shows a shield along with a sailing ship, a plow, and three sheaves of wheat. The ship stands for the commerce that developed by transporting goods by sea. The plow represents Pennsylvania's rich natural resources. The wheat symbolizes the state's fertile fields and the rich thought and action of its people. Above the shield is an eagle. Below the shield is a stalk of Indian corn and an olive branch. The back side of the seal shows a woman holding a sword and trampling on a lion. It bears the motto "Both Can't Survive." The woman represents liberty, and the lion stands for tyranny.

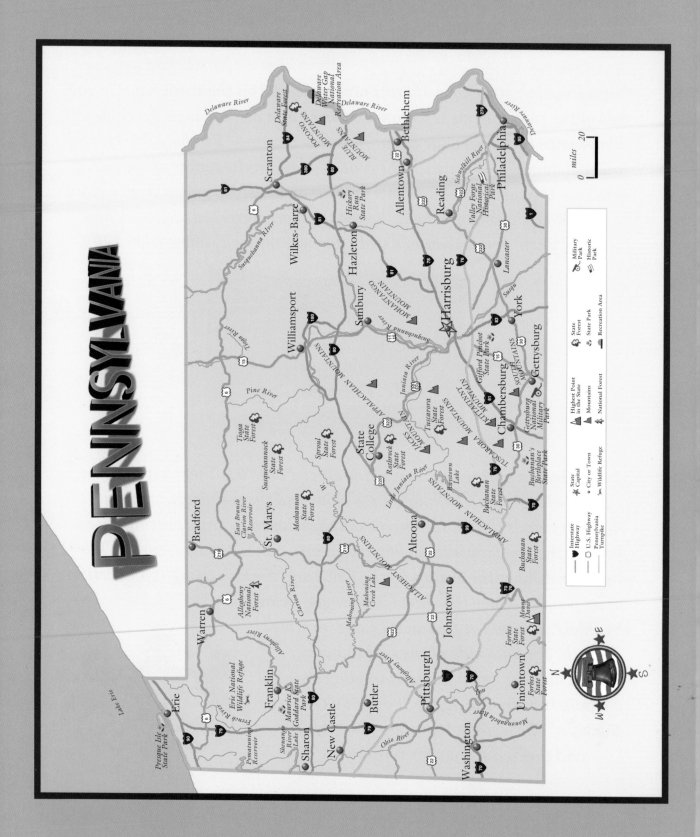

PENNSYLVANIA

State Song

Pennsylvania

words and music by Eddie Khoury
and Ronnie Bonner

PENN - SYL - VA - NIA, PENN - SYL - VA - NIA. Might - y is your

name, Steeped in glo - ry and tra - di - tion

Ob - ject of ac - claim, Where brave men fought the foe of

free - dom, Ty - ran - ny de - cried,

'Til the bell of in - de - pend - ence filled the coun - try -

side, PENN - SYL - VA - NIA, PENN - SYL - VA - NIA,

May your fu - ture be filled with hon - or

ev - er - last - ing as your his - to - ry.

MORE ABOUT PENNSYLVANIA

BOOKS

Hinman, Bonnie. *Pennsylvania: William Penn and the City of Brotherly Love*. Hockessin, DE: Mitchell Lane, 2007.

Seitz, Blair. *Pennsylvania: Yesterday & Today*. St. Paul, MN: Voyageur Press, 2007.

Staton, Hilarie. *Independence Hall*. New York: Chelsea House, 2010.

Wiener, Roberta, and James R. Arnold. *Pennsylvania: The History of Pennsylvania Colony, 1681-1776*. Chicago: Raintree, 2005.

Zavatsky, George, and Michele Zavatsky. *Kids Love Pennsylvania*. Powell, OH: Kids Love Publications, 2007.

WEBSITES

Explore PA History:
http://explorepahistory.com

Gettysburg National Military Park:
http://www.nps.gov/gett

PA.gov—the Official State Website:
http://www.pa.gov

Pennsylvania's Official Website for Tourism:
http://www.visitpa.com

Pennsylvania State Parks—Kid's Home Page:
http://www.dcnr.state.pa.us/stateparks/kids

Valley Forge National Historical Park:
http://www.nps.gov/vafo

Joyce Hart, whose grandparents came to Pennsylvania from Italy, has worked as an educator, an assistant librarian, an editor, and a desktop publisher. Currently she is a freelance writer and the author of several books. She has spent many years traveling the back roads of the United States.

Richard Hantula, based in New York, has worked as a writer and editor for more than three decades, during which he has crisscrossed Pennsylvania more times than he can remember.

INDEX

Page numbers in **boldface** are illustrations.